W HEN PRESIL
during his fii
doned Israel to the edicts of the United
Nations Security Council, he touched off a
furor about the failings of the U.N. itself. The
15-member council, tasked with securing
peace for the world, stood exposed as a col-
lection of bigots and hypocrites bent on pun-
ishing the only democracy in the Middle East.
This has inspired renewed calls from Congress and the American public to reform the
U.N., defund the U.N., withdraw from the
U.N. – calls for something salutary to be done.

The advent of a new administration opens
the door to a broader and urgently needed
debate over how, precisely, America in our
time should deal with the U.N. Created in
1945 by the victors of World War II with a
charter mission to "save succeeding genera-
tions from the scourge of war," the U.N. has
evolved into an organization notorious not
only for its waste but also for its abuse, fraud,
bigotry, mendacity, and predilection for

actions (or choreographed inactions) that make war more likely, not less.

The need for remedies goes way beyond the need to defang the Security Council's Resolution 2334 savaging Israel, a resolution that is both damaging and disingenuous. In the name of peace, and in the guise of condemning settlements, this resolution invites the world to further undermine an already beleaguered Jewish state. That's a road to war, not peace.

This diplomatic lynching is all the more alarming because it is no random act of prejudice, no appalling vice of an otherwise benevolent institution. It springs from a fundamental U.N. flaw that continually undermines not only Israel but the rest of the free world: the U.N.'s inherently corrupt moral compass. Combined with the U.N. system's privileges, immunities, proliferating ambitions, and ever-expanding overreach, this moral rot is a growing menace to America itself.

America's leaders have many means available to fight back, if they have the will to use

Combined with the U.N. system's privileges, immunities, proliferating ambitions, and ever-expanding overreach, this moral rot is a growing menace to America itself.

them. But if they confine their mission to yet another attempt to fix the U.N., they will fail. The desire to reform the U.N. rather than simply reject it, or at the very least work around it, springs from a worthy set of impulses, among them a basic prudence about being careful what you discard. However, there is by now a record of U.N. reform efforts stretching back decades – and it is horrifying. Among the more recent episodes was a big push in 2005–2006 to clean up the U.N. following the Oil-for-Food corruption scandal in Iraq, as well as congressional efforts in the

1990s to inspire better U.N. behavior by adding an internal audit department and withholding U.S. funds (a reform effort that failed to forestall the Oil-for-Food debacle).

Each time, the U.N. has emerged not only unreformed in character but bigger in scale, broader in reach, and at least as perverse, if not more so, in its influence and many of its activities. Emblematic of this pattern is the case of the old Commission on Human Rights, which the U.N. set up in 1946 "to weave the international legal fabric that protects our fundamental rights and freedoms." The commission became a magnet for human rights abusers among the U.N.'s member states, less interested in weaving the promised fabric than in redefining it to suit themselves. By 2003, the commission was packed with despotisms, focused chiefly on condemning Israel, and was chaired by Libya. The U.N.'s Potemkin remedy, in 2006, was to dissolve the commission and in its place set up the current Human Rights Council. A skeptical Bush administration steered clear of the new council, whereas Europe embraced it and Spain celebrated its nascence by donating a $23 million artwork ceiling, entailing more than 30 tons of paint, for its meeting chamber in Geneva. In 2009, despite evidence that the new council was already reverting to the vices of the old commission, the U.S. became a member under Obama's policy of engagement, proposing to work aggressively from within to make the council a world-class forum for advancing human rights. Today – you guessed it – the council is packed with human rights abusers fixated on condemning Israel.

It is time to consider quite seriously whether America should step clear of the U.N., withdrawing both U.S. money and the huge degree of legitimacy that America's founding membership and participation confers on the institution. The logistics of any such move might appear daunting, and the attendant uncertainties frightening. But for years, like the proverbial frog in a pot of water coming to a boil, America has been the mainstay of a

U.N. at which venally corrupt and morally malign behavior is a chronic near-certainty on an amplifying scale. That ought to qualify as even more daunting and frightening.

The clarifying question, too often ignored, is one of opportunity cost. If we did not have the U.N., what system, or set of coalitions, might America choose today to create in its place? What opportunities for life, liberty, and the pursuit of happiness have been choked off, around the globe, because the U.N. – thanks to the configuration of forces in 1945 – gave veto power on the Security Council to Stalin's Soviet Union, a privilege since inherited by an increasingly despotic and aggressive post-Soviet Russia?

For instance, would America, starting with a fresh slate, really invent or endorse as the world's leading human rights body an outfit that – à la U.N. Human Rights Council – routinely welcomes such members as Russia, China, Saudi Arabia, and Venezuela?

The task of unwinding the U.S. from its involvements in the U.N. might seem formidable. But at least for the sake of making informed judgments about the future of U.S. sovereignty, security, and foreign policy, surely it's worth working out how that might be done and what opportunities it might open up. There's little in the modern public domain to suggest that anyone versed in the byways of the U.N. has ever tackled the task of charting a full roadmap for such an exit.

It bears noting that the U.N. charter itself is hazy on such matters. The U.N.'s founders, mindful of the disintegration of its predecessor League of Nations, made no provision for the withdrawal of a member state. (Indonesia tried it in 1965, and then went back.) In principle, member states can be expelled. But that has not been the practice, although the U.N. charter's Chapter II, Article 6, states, "A Member of the United Nations which has persistently violated the Principles contained in the present Charter may be expelled from the Organization by the General Assembly upon the recommendation of the Security Council." That raises the question of why the likes of Iran, Sudan, and North Korea have not been kicked out. Surely they all qualify as being in violation of the charter obligations regarding "respect for human rights," and their commitments to any rational definition of peace are at best doubtful. If the U.N. doesn't take its own charter principles seriously, just how seriously should America take the U.N.?

These are matters ever more deserving of debate and in-depth exploration. President Trump and a number of Republican lawmakers are now pursuing ways of reducing America's support for the U.N. But among the policy elite of Washington and New York, any talk of actually leaving or massively defunding the U.N. has long been a no-go zone. It's been 34 years since the Cold War diplomatic fracas of the Reagan era in which Ambassador Jeane Kirkpatrick's deputy, Charles Lichenstein, dared to tell U.N. members that if they did not like the way America was treating them, they and the U.N. were welcome to leave; not only that but "the members of the

U.S. mission to the United Nations will be down at the dockside, waving you a fond farewell as you sail off into the sunset."

Today, in the wood-paneled realms of America's foreign-policy shamans, the 72-year-old U.N. ranks as a totem of international order, a permanent fixture, and – among select inner circles both within and surrounding the U.N. – a font of jobs, consulting contracts, influential connections, and per diems. Any attempt to suggest the U.N. might be past its shelf date invites being elbowed off the stage. The usual argument is that the U.N. may be imperfect, but it's all we've got.

America has been the mainstay of a U.N. at which venally corrupt and morally malign behavior is a chronic near-certainty.

The imperfections are by now so acute that the retort ought to be, If the U.N. is all we've got, it's time we came up with something else.

Long gone is the heady post–Cold War glow of the early 1990s, and gone with it should be any illusions that the U.N. is the vehicle to carry a post-Soviet brotherhood of man into a new golden age. That notion was eclipsed in short order by the genocidal slaughters of the mid-1990s, while U.N. peacekeepers looked on, in Rwanda and at Srebrenica. Any lingering faith in the U.N. as a guardian of world integrity should have been smothered by the global cloud of graft that mushroomed out of the U.N.'s 1996–2003 Oil-for-Food relief program for Saddam Hussein's U.N.-sanctioned Iraq.

Among the arguments today for carrying on with the U.N. is the idea that it was founded at the end of World War II with the main mission of averting another world war. And lo! In the 72 years since its founding there has been no global conflagration. Ergo, argue U.N. advocates, the U.N. prevents world war. There's a strong counter-argument that the U.N. is stealing credit from its often-reviled chief patron, the U.S. – the real mainspring of post–World War II peace and prosperity. The U.N.'s existence has coincided with that of the Pax Americana, in which the U.S. democratic superpower has stood – at least until recently – as leader of the free world, a bulwark of liberty, fighting a number of regional wars against aggressive tyrannies, quite plausibly deterring others, and winning the Cold War against a Soviet Union which, with considerable support inside the U.N., aspired to extend its communist blight around the globe. Arguably, America – and the NATO military alliance – won the Cold War despite the U.N., not because of it.

Obama, during his two terms as president, actually bolstered the case for American leadership and against the U.N.-as-world-peacekeeper, though presumably that was not his aim. For eight years, Obama effectively ordered America to stand down while he gave the U.N. every chance to display its prowess. Striving to place the U.N. at the center of America's foreign policy, he declared in a 2009 speech to the U.N. General Assembly that "no one nation can or should try to dominate another nation." He downsized the United States' role around much of the globe, gutting the U.S. military, pulling out of Iraq, deferring to Russia, bowing to China, inertly bearing witness to mass protests in Iran, erasing his own red line in Syria, and responding to videotaped beheadings by ISIS with the assurance that America stands "shoulder-to-shoulder" with the "international community."

Via the U.N., Obama led from behind on Libya, awaited U.N.-assisted diplomatic remedies as revolt in Syria exploded into all-out war, and on the way out of office capped his backseat endeavors by declining to wield the U.S. veto while the Security Council had its way with Israel. Obama also exalted the preferences of the U.N. over those of Congress, enlisting the U.N.'s eager help to clinch in the eyes of the "international community" such domestically unpopular "legacies" as the feckless Iran nuclear deal and the costly Paris climate agreement. In neither case did Obama submit his grand international bargain as a treaty, to be ratified by the Senate. Rather, he defaulted to the U.N., as an end run around the U.S. Constitution's system of checks and balances. In doing this, Obama provided a superb case study in how the U.N. allows national leaders to abuse their powers – supplanting even democratic process with the approval of a vast multilateral collective, accountable in theory to all nations and in practice to no one.

The results by now of letting the U.N. take the lead range from damaging to catastrophic. Around the world, according to Washington-based Freedom House, freedom is in its 10th straight year of an accelerating slide. Led-from-behind Libya has collapsed into a terrorist-infested failed state. In Syria's war, more than 400,000 people have died while refugees have swamped Europe and the ISIS "J.V." team has expanded into a global network engendering terrorist butcheries in venues such as – to name just a few – a Paris concert hall, a Brussels airport, and a San Bernardino Christmas party. Missile-testing, terrorist-sponsoring Iran is extending its reach in the Middle East. Russia has ripped the basic fabric of international order by snatching Crimea (and gotten away with it)

The usual argument is that the U.N. may be imperfect, but it's all we've got.

and threatens the rest of Ukraine. China is inventing territorial claims along vital shipping routes in the South China Sea. North Korea, despite a growing stack of U.N. sanctions and Obama's chairing of a "historic" 2009 U.N. Security Council meeting envisioning a world without nuclear weapons, has been openly building and testing nuclear weapons.

All these opportunistic players find at the U.N. a clubhouse convenient to their common antidemocratic, anti-American cause. In matters as troubling as nuclear proliferation or ballistic missile testing by rogue states, Russia and China make use of their veto power on the Security Council not for peace but for their own benefit. They either run interference for such client states as Iran and North Korea or extract concessions from the U.S. in exchange for approving sanctions that they then disregard – leaving it to the U.S. to chase after their illicit traffic. All the while, the entire U.N. enterprise is lavishly bankrolled and legitimized by the world's leading democracies, above all by the U.S., in the utopian hope that U.N. programs will bring prosperity and its powwows will bring peace.

In sum, welcome to the U.N. world order.

American voters seem less than delighted with these trends. Donald Trump won the presidency with a campaign that included a highly skeptical view of the U.N., blaming the organization for causing problems rather than solving them. He has criticized the U.N. as "just a club for people to get together, talk and have a good time." He has warned that unless the U.N. lives up to its "huge potential," it is "a waste of time and money."

That's a dramatic improvement over Obama's approach. But the U.N. does plenty of things far more pernicious than simply wasting time and money. And we should all be wary of the idea that the U.N., if only it could get its act together, has "huge potential." That's the endless *Through the Looking Glass* promise of jam tomorrow but – somehow – never jam today. It's an enticing view, especially for folks who might be too busy with their day jobs to pay much attention to the inner workings of the U.N. Many Americans are worried by the U.N.-adopted Iran nuclear deal, which paves Iran's path to the bomb and pads its pockets en route. But many also cherish childhood memories of collecting Halloween coins for UNICEF, the U.N.'s agency for children. The temptation is to figure that like most large families, the U.N. has its shortcomings, but at least it cares for children.

Yes, UNICEF, with its annual revenues of roughly $5 billion, does do some good for children. But what else goes on? The agency has a record of being close to tyrants and loose in its financial practices. For instance, among the 36 U.N. member states currently on the executive board, or governing body, of UNICEF is Iran – which still engages in juvenile executions (hanging being Tehran's preferred method). In 2009, UNICEF's Iran website featured a fundraising appeal for the children of terrorist-run Gaza, in which donors were invited to send money via an Iranian bank then under U.N. sanctions for its role in Iran's nuclear and missile programs. When I inquired at the time about this financial arrangement, UNICEF would not disclose what was going on with that bank account. Also on the current UNICEF board are such human rights abusers as Belarus,

Russia, Saudi Arabia, Cuba, and China – home until just last year to a longtime one-child policy that included fines and forced abortions.

If America wants to help the world's children, a highly relevant question is whether there might be better ways to do it than via an opaque U.N. agency with dictators serving on its board. Were a private American charity to try transferring funds to terrorist-run Gaza via a bank blacklisted as a conduit for illicit nuclear and missile traffic, it's likely that someone would land in jail. But when the U.N. does it, it's just another day raising money for children.

That's pretty much how it works across the entire U.N. system, where UNICEF's despot-infested board is basically business as usual. Iran, in all its misogyny, also currently sits on the executive board of U.N. Women and in 2009 chaired the board of the U.N.'s flagship agency, the U.N. Development Program. From 2012 to 2016, despite being under U.N. sanctions for most of that stretch, Iran chaired the second-largest voting bloc in the General Assembly: the 120-member Non-Aligned Movement (NAM). Last year Venezuela succeeded Iran as head of NAM, hosting a party at which only a handful of political eminences showed up, but among them were the presidents of Iran, Zimbabwe, and Cuba; the titular head of state of North Korea, Kim Yong-nam; and the head of the Palestinian Authority, Mahmoud Abbas.

The assembly's largest voting bloc, the development-themed 134-member group known as the G-77, distinguished itself in 2009 by choosing as its chair the ambassador of Sudan. Sudan's president, Omar al-Bashir, had been charged four years earlier by the International Criminal Court for genocide and crimes against humanity (al-Bashir, still Sudan's president, has never been arrested). Secretary-General Ban Ki-moon sent Sudan's ambassador his best wishes, and Sudan celebrated its ascent to the head of the G-77 by throwing a party in the U.N. Delegates' Dining Room, replete, as reported by *Inner*

City Press, with ice sculptures, lobster, and chocolate-covered strawberries.

All of which brings us to the core design flaws of the U.N. itself.

To the casual visitor, the U.N. might look and sound like a grand experiment in global democracy, dedicated to liberty and justice for all. Under the 1945 charter, with its talk of peace and freedom, the U.N. holds elections. Its 193-member General Assembly votes, upon recommendation of the Security Council, for a secretary-general who routinely makes way for a successor, after serving one or two five-year terms. The 15-member Security Council often holds votes, albeit with five permanent members – Russia, China, France, Britain, and the U.S. – wielding the power to veto any resolution.

But the U.N. is not a democratic polity. Its leaders, or officials, are not accountable to those truly affected by its actions. It is a huge collective of governments, which in effect reports to itself. There is no constituency of ordinary people who can vote its officials out

The U.N.'s existence has coincided with that of the Pax Americana.

or hold them directly responsible for what they do. There is no equivalent of public confirmation hearings for the appointment of senior officials. There is no provision for draft Security Council resolutions to be disclosed to the public before they are introduced for a vote.

To make matters worse, the U.N. was created with a shield of diplomatic privileges and immunities. That has its conveniences for the U.N., but for the rest of us it means there is no way to legally hold its offices, personnel, or programs to account. Were the U.N. merely a talking shop, these immunities might be reasonable. There is a long tradition of envoys enjoying immunity to come parley. But the U.N. long ago outgrew the role of a mere council. Today it more closely resembles a neocolonial empire, with overlapping and intersecting offices, programs, peacekeepers, special initiatives, and ambitions to try to engineer development and regulate the climate of the planet. This goes on around the globe, across borders and legal jurisdictions, swaddled in laissez-passer privilege and diplomatic immunities. This arrangement fosters what a U.N. internal auditor neatly summarized back in 2006 – while investigating massive corruption in U.N. peacekeeping contracts – as a "culture of impunity." The secretary-general has the power in special circumstances to waive immunity, but such instances are rare.

In other words, while proposing to act as moral arbiter and shepherd of peace and prosperity for the planet, the U.N. is itself exempt from law and justice. These immunities also translate into a considerable degree of secrecy at the U.N., which cranks out endless information on its labors for humanity but has no compelling incentive to answer questions it doesn't like. In 2006, following a number of huge bribery scandals involving senior U.N. staff, the U.N. Secretariat rolled out an "ethics" reform involving financial disclosure by senior U.N. officials – with the intriguing feature that these officials could opt not to disclose their disclosures to the public.

To make it still worse, within this secretive and diplomatically immune collective, the majority of member states are not free polities. They bring with them an antidemocratic tilt that permeates the U.N. According to a 2016 report by Freedom House, only about 40 percent of the world's population and 44 percent of its countries rank as free – a database that roughly duplicates the membership of the U.N. The rest of the world lives under governments that range from "partly free," such as Guatemala or Pakistan, to "not free," such as Cuba or North Korea. That's the voting majority in the General Assembly.

At the U.N., the effect of this mix of dictatorships and democracies is to create a rough set of double standards regarding who takes seriously the U.N.'s edicts and ground rules and who doesn't. American administrations, bound by American law and answerable to voters, pretty much have to keep their official bargains with the U.N., or justify to the satisfaction of those back home why they didn't. Dictators, when they're at home, get to call the shots, and tend to silence anyone who dissents. They are much freer to pick and choose which U.N. constraints they will honor and which they won't. The upshot is that while law-abiding, free societies bear the full cost of whatever they agree to at the U.N., dictatorships have every incentive to manipulate and exploit the U.N. system to the hilt.

Thus, for instance, the U.S. may woo and reward China's agreement to approve a U.N. sanctions resolution meant to stop North Korean nuclear tests. But when it comes to enforcing those sanctions, different rules seem to apply. America tends to prosecute violators. China, for all its amazing surveillance apparatus, can't locate them.

There's yet another layer to this setup, fraught with yet more perverse incentives, concerning the matter of legitimacy. U.N. membership confers a seat and one vote in the General Assembly on all countries alike, whether they are democracies or dictatorships. For democratic governments, which derive their legitimacy from voters back home, this is useful but not necessarily earthshaking. Dictators, however, who tend to rule through a mix of force and propaganda, are forever in search of a legitimacy they do not actually enjoy at home. U.N. membership dignifies them with seats alongside the world's freely elected governments and treats them all as equals. When tyrants or their ministers parade across the U.N. stage in New York at the General Assembly opening every September, sandwiched between the speakers from America, Britain, and Japan, before a golden backdrop, one of the implicit messages to their oppressed populations back home is that their rulers, in the eyes of the world, are legitimate. An epitome of this

Obama provided a superb case study in how the U.N. allows national leaders to abuse their powers.

moral equivalence was the U.N.'s decision in 1991 to admit simultaneously as members the countries of North and South Korea – welcoming as twins a totalitarian state and a vibrant developing democracy.

Advocates of the U.N. like to argue that it provides the U.S. with a brand of global legitimacy and latitude it would not otherwise enjoy. Actually, it's the other way around. It is primarily the U.S. that confers legitimacy on the U.N. On balance, the U.N. offers far more benefits at the margin to despotisms than it does to its democratic chief patrons. The U.N. effectively serves as a vehicle for the transfer of legitimacy from democratic to unfree regimes, dignifying the dictators and tainting the complicit democrats. Presumably that's at least one of the reasons why, when Deputy Ambassador Lichenstein in 1983 invited the U.N. (and the Soviet delegation in particular) to sail off into the sunset, nobody sailed.

Into this stew of self-dealing member states, the taxpayers of the world's leading democracies pour tens of billions every year. America is by far the largest contributor, paying for 22 percent of the General Assembly's annual budget and more than 28 percent of the peacekeeping budget, for a combined sum that currently comes to roughly $3 billion. You might suppose that America's billions buy plenty of influence over how that money gets spent. But long custom at the U.N. has largely turned America's outsized contributions into an entitlement. A telling moment came during a General Assembly debate in December 2007 over the assembly's proposed budget, to which the U.S. had some objections. These budgets are usually passed by consensus, but on this occasion, the U.S. asked for a vote. Following an all-night debate, during which some members left, the assembly approved the budget, by a vote of 142 to 1. That lone dissenting vote was cast by the biggest donor in the room, the United States.

Most debates about funding or defunding the U.N. tend to focus on the U.S. dues to the General Assembly and peacekeeping. But that $3 billion is just a fraction of the lucre that the American government gives to the wider U.N. system. Some years ago, during a bout of U.N. reform following the Oil-for-Food scandal, Congress began requiring the administration's Office of Management and Budget (OMB) to provide yearly reports on total U.S. contributions to the U.N., across the entire federal government. These reports were illuminating, showing U.S. tax dollars flowing to the U.N. not only via the State Department but from 10 other departments, including Agriculture, Commerce, Energy, and Health and Human Services, plus outfits such as the Environmental Protection

Agency. For fiscal year 2010, the total reported by OMB was $7.69 billion – billions more than the dues for the General Assembly's "core" budget and peacekeeping.

Regrettably, the congressional require-ment for these OMB reports expired some years ago, and after 2011 the Obama adminis-tration stopped releasing them. Fiscal year 2010 is the most recent for which these offi-cial compilations of total U.S. contributions to the U.N. are publicly available. But some information can be gleaned from the U.N. website, where the most recent available fig-ures show that by 2014, total U.S. contribu-tions totaled $10 billion (more than three times the amount America contributes to the "core" U.N. budget plus peacekeeping). That $10 billion represents about one-fifth of the U.N.'s systemwide revenues for 2014, which, as reported on the same U.N. website, totaled a staggering $48 billion.

It's hard to know how reliable or genu-inely comprehensive these U.N. numbers are, or what lags might be reflected in the figures.

The U.S. reports in fiscal years, the U.N. in calendar years. For fiscal year 2010, the U.S. administration reported giving the U.N. a few billion more ($7.69 billion) than the U.N. says it received from the U.S. government for either calendar year 2010 ($5.0 billion) or calendar year 2011 ($4.6 billion). In early January, the U.N. website showed total systemwide revenues spiking in 2012 by tens of billions for a total of $83.7 billion; when I queried the U.N. spokesman's office about that amount, the U.N. revised the figure on its website down to $42.3 billion, attributing the much higher sum shown earlier to "data not displaying correctly."

Errors and discrepancies are nothing unusual in matters involving U.N. financial reporting. A U.N. system that began as a club of dues-paying governments has become a global fundraising franchise so complex that the U.N. itself seems to have trouble keeping track. There are voluntary donations from governments, donations from nongovernmental organizations, donations in kind, public-private partnerships, and a welter of obscure trust funds and special appeals – along with those coins collected for UNICEF.

Whatever the actual sums, it's safe to say that many billions of U.S. dollars flow annually into the vast global conglomerate that is the U.N. system, with its dictator-laced governing boards and biases and its diplomatically immune personnel and ventures. For the U.N., the incentive is to keep discovering new roles for itself, conducive to yet more fundraising, chiefly from governments. The U.N. is flagrantly failing in such charter missions as ending war in the Middle East or preventing nuclear proliferation by North Korea. But it has done quite well for itself out of proposing to regulate the climate of the planet, at some date in the misty distant future, to within a few decimal points centigrade of some bureaucratically beatified target temperature.

There are plenty of caveats about how well the U.N.'s ever-expanding galaxy of programs serves the U.N.'s officially chosen beneficiaries, such as the children guarded by peacekeepers or underwritten by UNICEF. But there is little doubt that for a privileged few, the U.N.'s franchise as prime official guardian of the world order translates into a U.N. gravy train, transferring wealth (and jobs) from ordinary taxpayers to officials of the U.N. and their counterparts within the policy elites of the U.N. member states.

To help keep U.S. funds flowing in, the U.N. maintains an information office in Washington, surrounded by a growing cluster of U.N. agency liaison offices, all located on or near Washington's K Street – a venue famous for its lobbyists and close to the wellsprings of congressional appropriations and administration approval. Officially these U.N. offices are in Washington to provide information, taking their cue from the 1946 founding mission of the U.N.'s Department of Information: "to promote global awareness and understanding of the work of the United Nations." In practice, the U.N. tends to hire former U.S. State Department and congressional staffers to run these offices, whence they can elaborate to their former colleagues and connections, both on the Hill and at the State Department, on the U.N.'s self-described virtues and need for ever more U.S. tax dollars.

The majority of member states are not free polities. They bring with them an antidemocratic tilt that permeates the U.N.

As a rule, the U.N. does not like to promote awareness of the incentives driving its own Department of Information. But in trying to winnow U.N. facts from fiction, it can be useful to keep in mind that the U.N.'s information department reports to the General Assembly's Committee on Information, which includes among its 115 members such paragons of propaganda as North Korea, China,

Syria, Sudan, and Cuba, with Iran currently serving – and not for the first time – as the committee's rapporteur. The information department, overseen by this committee, is funded out of the General Assembly budget to the tune of roughly $100 million per year, with 22 percent of that money coming from the United States. In sum, money being fungible, this means that the U.N., via information offices overseen in part by some of the world's worst regimes, spends American money to lobby in Washington for yet more American money.

Out of the U.N. murk, scandals routinely arise, many of them appalling in their dimensions but quickly gone from the headlines. U.N. secrecy, spin, and immunities often mean that the full story never gets aired and no one gets called to account. More than a decade after the U.N. proclaimed a policy of "zero tolerance" for peacekeepers raping children they are sent to protect, the U.N. has still not managed to stop such abominations – though these days it does provide generic statistics on the problem. Meantime, peacekeepers are dispatched to places where there is no peace to keep, such as South Sudan. Or, like the peacekeepers of the U.N. Interim Force in Lebanon (UNIFIL) watching the terrorists of Hezbollah truck in weapons – again – for the next war against Israel, the U.N.'s blue berets provide a facade of control while under their gaze the preparations proceed for slaughter.

For a saga that showcased myriad U.N. failings, it's worth revisiting the 2007 scandal that became known as Cash for Kim. That geyser of sleaze erupted out of the Pyongyang office of the U.N.'s flagship agency, the U.N. Development Program (UNDP). A whistleblower who worked in that office tipped off U.S. authorities that in North Korea the UNDP, in violation of the U.N.'s own rules, had developed much too cozy a relationship with the tyrannical regime of North Korea. As it turned out, the UNDP office was dishing out funds to the North Korean government, importing U.S.-government-controlled items that could be put to dual use for weapons technology, allowing North Koreans to handle the UNDP's bank account, transferring funds to proliferation-connected business entities in Asia, and keeping counterfeit U.S. $100 bills in its office safe. There was a U.N. inquiry, and for a while the UNDP office in Pyongyang was shut down. But the only person punished was the whistleblower, who lost his job.

This took place under the aegis of a U.N. agency tasked with "development," which brings us to yet another piece of the U.N. problem. Presumably there are some good intentions behind such U.N. cross-agency grand plans for the planet as the 2030 Agenda for Development, with its "17 Sustainable Development Goals." But if there's a whiff of the old Soviet five-year plans to this lingo, it's no accident. These huge U.N. programs, laying out blueprints for the erstwhile benefit of humanity, basically amount to central planning. It's entirely fitting that the U.N. chose as its new secretary-general António Guterres, who has not only served as a prime minister of Portugal and head of the U.N.'s refugee agency, but whose credentials also include a six-year stint as head of the Socialist International. This does not bode well.

The experiments of the last century should have taught us that central planning is a recipe not for development but for poverty and authoritarian rule. The real remedy is freedom: democracy, under decent and impartial law, coupled with free markets. But that goes against the grain of the U.N. character described above, and for the fundraising purposes of the U.N., there's not much money in it. So the U.N.'s grand plans continue to multiply, often to the benefit of the rotating arrays of dictatorships that sit on the U.N.'s governing bodies. It is perhaps telling that at the time of the UNDP's Cash for Kim scandal, North Korea had a seat on the UNDP executive board, and the U.N. was paying to fly North Korea's envoys, business class, to the UNDP's board meetings in New York.

Likewise, the U.N.'s enormous agenda

focused on "climate change" boils down, in economic terms, to a grab for control of the vast energy sector of the world economy, or at least a big say in how it works. Whatever your views on climate change, the further question ought to be whether the U.N. – immune, opaque, and unaccountable – is remotely qualified to regulate anything. This is an institution that can't keep track of its own money, and based on the record sometimes prefers not to.

For America's leaders, the temptation is simply to live with the failings of the U.N. (imperfect, but all we've got) or to try to address the worst of them, case by case, again and again. The results, on balance, just keep getting more dangerous, more corrupt, more ruinous. It's time to look for alternatives. The essence of freedom is choice. A basic element of the democracy and capitalism that made America great is competition. Are things really that different in world affairs?

It's time to end the U.N.'s 72-year monopoly as the world's leading multilateral body.

How that might be done needs serious study. But the first step is to bring the question fully into the debate. Where to begin?

The first priority should be to scrap the Washington taboos, by asking not whether America should pull down the pillars of the U.N. but how that might most beneficially be done and what better could be built or

---

It is a huge collective of governments, which in effect reports to itself.

---

devised in its place. Some inspiration could perhaps be taken from John F. Kennedy's famous line about choosing to do such things as go to the moon "not because they are easy, but because they are hard."

For an exit plan from the U.N. to succeed, there must be – to begin with – a plan. This is something that men of good will could surely come up with. It would help to hear from experts versed in the ways of the U.N. and Washington but not invested in them. It would also help to have a genuine debate about what America would need, and could create, were it to jettison the U.N., in order to navigate an increasingly dangerous 21st century.

To better inform any such planning, it would help to have current information, in full, on what the U.S. actually provides to the U.N. The Trump administration could revive the practice of releasing comprehensive OMB reports on all U.S. contributions, and provide to Congress and the public the information that has gone unreported from fiscal year 2011 to the present. Congress, for its part, could revive its requirement for such reports.

It would also be useful to have a clearer window on the U.N. itself, with an eye to asking if there are better ways to help the world than via the likes of UNICEF, the UNDP, and the General Assembly. In 2007, when the Cash for Kim scandal hit the headlines during Ban Ki-moon's first month as secretary-general, Ban's immediate reaction was to promise, via his press office, that he would "call for an urgent, system wide and external inquiry into all activities done around the globe by the U.N. funds and programs." Within days, Ban scrapped that promise. The urgently needed global, independent audit of the U.N. system never took place. It is a pledge that his newly arrived successor, Guterres, should be asked to redeem (with a truly independent audit of the U.N. Secretariat thrown in). Trump, who has now taken ownership of America's relations with the U.N., would be wise to insist on it. If Guterres and his U.N. colleagues say no, then that too is informative.

The U.N. is swift to tout its own achievements, real or imagined. But there is plenty in the record to suggest that the more we understand about the true workings of the U.N., the stronger the case for consigning it to the heap of failed collectivist experiments of the 20th century and for designing better alternatives. Either this task gets done in the not-so-distant future because men of vision and good will put their minds to finding ways to do it, or it waits upon the aftermath of some cataclysm, toward which the U.N., as now configured, increasingly impels us.

First American edition published in 2017 by Encounter Books,
an activity of Encounter for Culture and Education, Inc.,
a nonprofit, tax exempt corporation.
Encounter Books website address: www.encounterbooks.com

Manufactured in the United States and printed on
acid-free paper. The paper used in this publication meets
the minimum requirements of ANSI/NISO Z39.48–1992
(R 1997) (*Permanence of Paper*).

FIRST AMERICAN EDITION

LIBRARY OF CONGRESS
CATALOGING-IN-PUBLICATION DATA
IS AVAILABLE